NICKELODEON®

SpongeBob squarepants™

GONE JELLYFISHING

TITAN BOOKS

SPONGEBOB SQUAREPANTS: GONE JELLYFISHING

ISBN-10: 1 84576 223 1
ISBN-13: 9781845762230

Stories & Scripts: Kent Osborne, Ted Couldron, Paul Tibbitt, C. H. Greenblatt, Kaz, Walt Dohm, Derek Drymon, Sam Henderson, Sherm Cohen & Johnny Ryan
Pencils & Inks: Gregg Schigiel, Jay Lender, Sherm Cohen, C. H. Greenblatt, Tony Millionaire, Mark O'Hare, Derek Kirk Kim, Scott Roberts, Vince Deporter, Kazu Kibuishi & Dave Cooper
Colours: Sno Cone Studios, Nick Jennings, Tom Luth, Digital Chameleon & Derek Kirk Kim
Letters: Comicraft, Sherm Cohen, C. H. Greenblatt, Tony Millionaire, Derek Kirk Kim, Vince Deporter & Jay Lender

Published by Titan Books,
a division of Titan Publishing Group Ltd.
144 Southwark St
London SE1 0UP

A CIP catalogue record for this title is available from the British Library.

This edition first published: November 2005

3 5 7 9 10 8 6 4

Printed in Italy.

Also available from Titan:
The Powerpuff Girls: Go, Girls, Go! (ISBN: 1 84023 885 2)
The Powerpuff Girls: To The Rescue (ISBN: 1 84023 886 0)
Star Wars Clone Wars Adventures Vol. 1 (ISBN: 1 84023 995 6)
Star Wars Clone Wars Adventures Vol. 2 (ISBN: 1 84023 840 2)
Star Wars Clone Wars Adventures Vol. 3 (ISBN: 1 84576 020 4)
Star Wars Clone Wars Adventures Vol. 4 (ISBN: 1 84576 189 8)

What did you think of this book? We love to hear from our readers. Please email us at: readerfeedback@titanemail.com, or write to us at the above address. You can also visit us at www.titanbooks.com

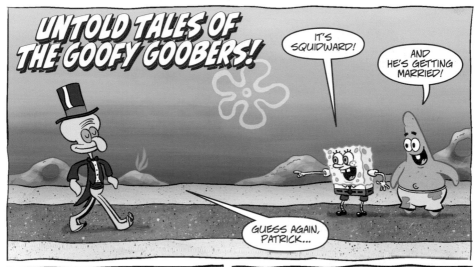

UNTOLD TALES OF THE GOOFY GOOBERS!

IT'S SQUIDWARD!

AND HE'S GETTING MARRIED!

GUESS AGAIN, PATRICK...

I HAPPEN TO HAVE FRONT-ROW SEATS TO THE BIKINI BOTTOM SYMPHONY.

CONCERT HALL
goofy Goober's

WHAT THE--?

GOOFY GOOBER'S

CONCERT HALL
goofy Goober's

LOOK, SQUIDWARD! THEY TORE DOWN THE CONCERT HALL.

AND PUT UP THIS FANCY SIGN.

NOW WHAT DO I DO?

DON'T WORRY, SQUIDWARD! WE'LL GO IN AND GIVE THEM A PIECE OF YOUR MIND!

YEAH! WE'LL MAKE THEM REGRET MESSING WITH OUR PAL SQUIDWARD.

OKAY, MARCH RIGHT IN THERE AND TELL THEM THAT NO ONE ASKED FOR THEIR *FUN RESTAURANT*, AND IF THEY *HAD* ASKED I WOULD HAVE POINTED OUT THAT NOTHING IS MORE FUN THAN BEING EXPOSED TO GREAT CULTURAL WORKS LIKE...

GOTCHA!

...AND THAT SOMETHING SO JUVENILE AS A TALKING PEANUT COULD NEVER COMPARE WITH THE SOPHISTICATED BALANCE OF WIND PERCUSSION COMBINED...

RIGHT ON!

AHEM. WE'D LIKE TO SPEAK TO THE MANAGER OF THIS ESTABLISHMENT.

RIGHT AWAY, SIR.

TICK TICK — TICK TICK TICK

WELL, WE WAITED A WHOLE TEN SECONDS.

LET'S GO FIND HIM.

BUT ONCE INSIDE...

LOOK, SPONGEBOB! THEY HAVE STRAW HATS!

AND THEY HAVE GAMES OF CHANCE!

AND AN ANIMATRONIC JUG BAND FEATURING GOOFY GOOBER AND THE NUTTY JUNCTION CROONERS!

AND ALL THEY SERVE IS ICE CREAM!!!

YOU GENTLEMEN HAD SOMETHING TO TELL THE MANAGER?

≋AHEM≋ YES, WE DO!

YEAH, TELL HIM! TELL HIM!

PARENT ZONE

NO! NO! NO! THEY'RE SUPPOSED TO BE GIVING THEM A PIECE OF MY MIND...

...NOT GIVING IN TO...

...UH...DELICIOUS-LOOKING...UH... SCRUMPTIOUS...

...ICE CREAM!

PARENT ZONE

SLUUURP

HEY, OLD MAN, NO LICKING THE GLASS!

BUT I WANT ICE CREAM.

THEN GO GET A JOB AND BUY SOME. THOSE MT. RAZZLEBERRYS ARE FOR KIDS ONLY!

PARENTS JUST DON'T GET IT.

WELL, TOPPY, LOOKS LIKE I HAD YOU DRY-CLEANED FOR NOTHING.

THANKS FOR GIVING THEM A PIECE OF MY MIND!

CHEER UP, SQUIDWARD. WE WON YOU THIS PRIZE AT SKEE-BALL.

AND IT ONLY COST US $200 IN TOKENS!

A TOY CLARINET? WOW! THANKS, FELLAS!

HEY, YA KNOW, MY KID WON ME THIS KEY CHAIN THAT PLAYS REAL PIANO SOUND EFFECTS.

AND MY KID LEFT HIS EMPTY SODA BOTTLE.

GOOFY, GOOFY, GOOBER, GOOBER, YEAH!

THE END

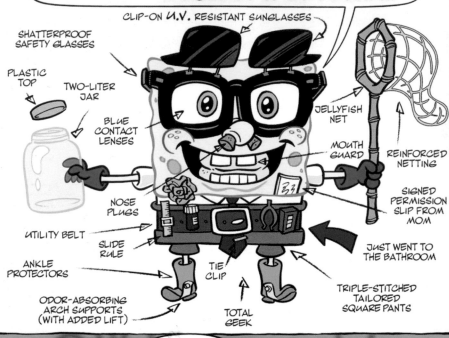

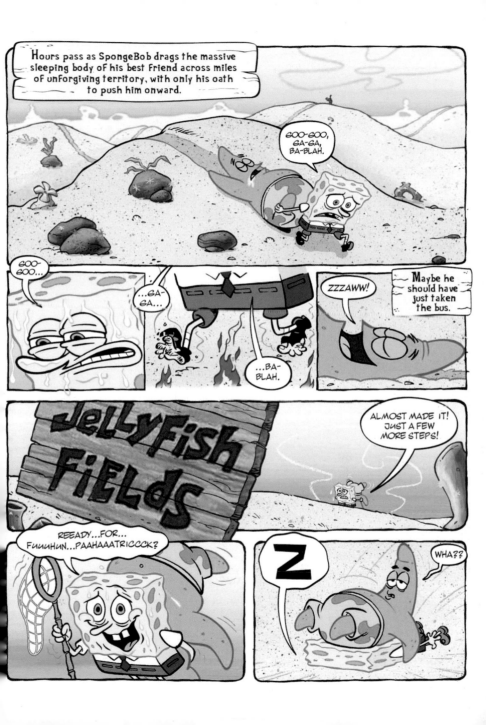

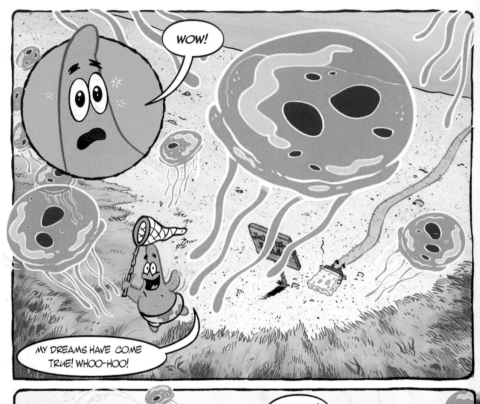

Hours later, night falls on JellyFish Fields...

ZZZ--NIGHT?!

THAT MEANS I SLEPT THROUGH THE WHOLE DAY! I MISSED ALL THE JELLY!

I WONDER WHAT COULD HAVE HAPPENED TO...

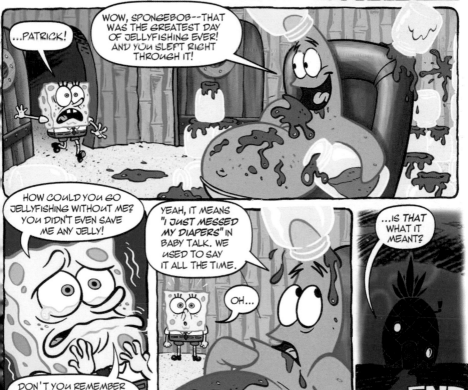

...PATRICK!

WOW, SPONGEBOB--THAT WAS THE GREATEST DAY OF JELLYFISHING EVER! AND YOU SLEPT RIGHT THROUGH IT!

HOW COULD YOU GO JELLYFISHING WITHOUT ME? YOU DIDN'T EVEN SAVE ME ANY JELLY!

DON'T YOU REMEMBER WHAT GOO-GOO, GA-GA, BA-BLAH MEANS?

YEAH, IT MEANS "I JUST MESSED MY DIAPERS" IN BABY TALK. WE USED TO SAY IT ALL THE TIME.

OH...

...IS THAT WHAT IT MEANT?

END

Princess Mindy in Fin Doctor

Don't forget to keep that bandage dry...

...and check back in one week!

Next!

⌐Gasp!⌐

Mindy! What is the *meaning* of this-- this *charity*?

Daddy, these sea creatures are *sick!* We've *got* to help them!

SNAP!

sneak sneak

Bah! I don't care if they get *fin-fluenza* and their *fins* fall off!

They're here to serve *us*, not the other way around!

But, *Dad*...

Don't care if their fins fall off, eh? Hmm...

The next day...

A little *service* here?!!

Your ruler *awaits!!!*

Yoo-hoo!

Grrr... Where *are* those good-for-nothing *servants*...?

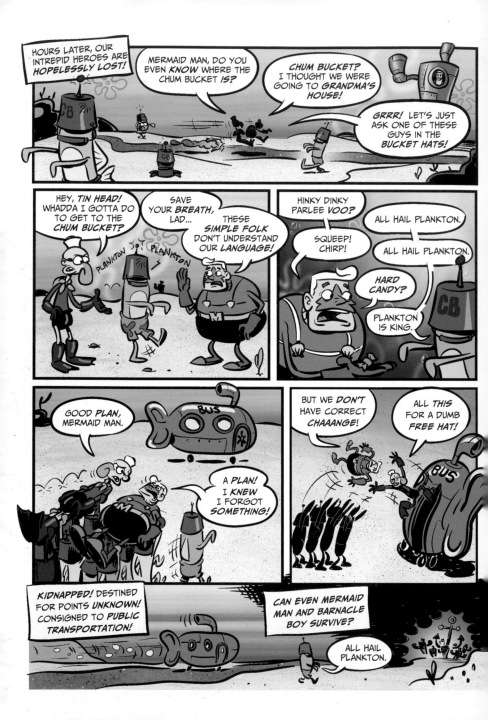

MOMENTS LATER...

OPEN UP! I COMMAND YOU TO OPEN THIS DOOR!

BINK BINK

BINK

WELL, A BIG HELLO TO—

AHEM!

OH! HEY, PATRICK!

YES, THAT'S RIGHT! I'M YOUR STUPID FRIEND, PATRICK!

BUT WE SHOULD BE OKAY. IT'S NOT AGGRESSIVE...

...TO ANYTHING BIGGER THAN A PLANKTON.

WOW! I'VE NEVER SEEN ONE THIS CLOSE!

ZAP

NEAT! THAT MUST BE THE VENOM SAC!

ZAP

I'VE READ THAT IT EVEN HAS STINGERS ON ITS STINGERS!

ZAP

HEY! NOW IT'S SLAPPING YOU! I DIDN'T KNOW IT COULD DO THAT!

ZAP

I THINK IT'S DONE. OH, WAIT...

ZAP

NOW IT'S DONE.

THAT WAS INCREDIBLE, PATRICK!

AND SO...

YEP. WE'RE JUST TWO BEST FRIENDS, WALKING AND TALKING.

SAY, I'VE GOT A FUN IDEA FOR A GAME!

IT'S CALLED "LET'S TELL EACH OTHER SECRETS"! YOU GO FIRST! WHAT'S THE KRABBY PATTY FORMULA?

SORRY, PATRICK. WHAT WAS THAT? I WAS SINGING A SONG IN MY HEAD CALLED "SINGING LOUD."

WANNA HEAR IT?

NOT REALLY.

SINGING LOUD! SINGING LOUD! IF YOU MEAN IT, YOU GOTTA SCREAM IT! SINGING LOUD! SINGING LOUD! IF YOU MEAN IT, YOU GOTTA SCREAM IT!

...AND YOU'VE GOT YOURSELF A JUICY, CRUSTY, GREASY PILE OF *HEART-STOPPING MORNING MADNESS!*

'CAUSE EATING KRABBY PATTIES FOR EVERY MEAL JUST ISN'T *HEALTHY!*

DON'T WORRY, GARY. I DIDN'T FORGET ABOUT YOU.

GARY

Meow?

WELL, I NEED A BIGGER BREAKFAST THAN YOU -- I'VE GOT A BIG DAY OF WORK AHEAD OF ME!

TELL YOU WHAT -- WHEN YOU START COOKING, YOU CAN CHOOSE THE MENU. HA-HA!

GARY

THE KRUSTY KRAB

LATER...

DING DING!

ORDER UP!

ENTER

ORDER UH --

WOW! PATRICK!

WHERE'D YOU GET ALL THE NIFTY GEWGAWS?

THE CARNIVAL'S IN TOWN TODAY! AND I GOT ALL THIS STUFF, AND I ATE POPCORN AND HOT DOGS AND COTTON CANDY...

... AND AFTER I RODE ON THE SPIN-OUT, I GOT TO EAT ALL THAT STUFF AGAIN!

BUT THE CREAM DE LA CHEESE IS THIS COMMEMORABLE *MERMAID MAN* KEWPIE DOLL I GOT FOR SURVIVING "MERMAID MAN'S TUNNEL OF EVIL"!

BLAH BLAH BLAH CANDY BLAH BLAH BLAH CAROUSEL BLAH BLAH BLAH RINGTOSS BLAH BLAH BLAH

TOO BAD YOU'RE WORKING, CAUSE THE CARNIVAL'S ONLY HERE IN TOWN FOR ONE...

...DAY!

KRASH!

TEN MINUTES LATER...

Plot: Paul Tibbet. Script, art, and lettering: Sherm Cohen. Coloring: Digital Chameleon. Special thanks to: Stephen Hillenburg and Derek Drymon.

GEE, THANKS, SQUIDWARD!

HEH, HEH... SUCKER!

HIC! CRASH HIC! BOOM HIC! BASH

HIC!

OH, NO! ≥SOB≥ LOOK WHAT YOU DID TO GLASSY!

I'M SORRY, SQUIDWARD, BUT YOUR IDEA DIDN'T WORK! HIC! DO YOU HAVE ANY OTHER IDEAS?

YES! GO BOTHER PATRICK!

HIC!

AND SO...

THE BEST THING TO DO IS TO STAND ON YOUR TONGUE AND HOLD YOUR BREATH.

LIGE YITH?

HIC!

AW, TARTAR SAUCE! I'LL NEVER GET RID OF THESE HICCUPS!

OH! YOU HAVE THE HICCUPS?

WELL, HIC! WHAT DID YOU THINK I SAID?

I THOUGHT YOU SAID YOU HAVE THE HICCUPS.

I DO HAVE THE HIC! HICCUPS!

OH, WELL, THE BEST THING TO DO IS TO STAND ON YOUR TONGUE...

NEVER MIND!

DID YOU STAND ON YOUR TONGUE? YES!

DID YOU DUST SQUIDWARD'S SHELVES? YES!

HOW ABOUT LAUNDRY DETERGENT?

YES! YES! HICCUP!

I'VE TRIED THEM ALL!

WELL, IT LOOKS LIKE THERE'S ONLY ONE THING LEFT TO DO...

YOU'LL HAVE TO TAKE A TRIP TO...

HICCUP ISLAND

"HICCUP HICCUP! ISLAND"?

NO! NOT "HICCUP HICCUP ISLAND," JUST "HICCUP ISLAND."

LOOK HERE.

EVER SINCE PHLEGMY McWELTERSON CAUSED THE WRECK OF THE S.S. GLOTTIS, IT'S BEEN THE CUSTOM OF THE SEA TO BANISH ALL HICCUPPING SAILORS TO THIS ISLAND OF LOST SOULS.

Isle of the Hiccup

HICCUP!

BUT I'M NOT A SAILOR, MR. KRABS... I'M A FRY COOK!

AYE... THAT'S WHAT PHLEGMY McWELTERSON SAID, TOO.

C'MON, LAD... I'LL TAKE YOU THERE MYSELF.

"The Hole at the Bottom of the Sea"

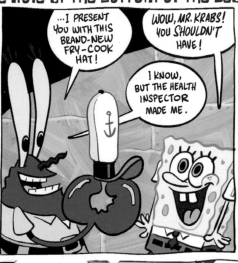

Story, art, and lettering: Sherm Cohen. Coloring: Digital Chameleon. *SpongeBob SquarePants* created by Stephen Hillenburg. Special thanks to Stu Chaifetz.

AND SO, BACK AT THE BOTTOM...

NO ONE ROBS FROM OUR SACRED SHRINE AND LIVES!

HOW DARE YOU STEAL ONE OF THE GIFTS FROM ABOVE!

NOW, STRANGERS... FEEL THE WRATH OF OUR KING!

BUT, YOUR HIGHNESS... THAT'S NOT A HOLY RELIC! IT'S JUST MY HAT THAT FELL DOWN THE HOLE!

I KNOW NOT THIS WORD "HAT" THAT YOU SPEAK...

...BUT THIS SURE MAKES A NIFTY COVER FOR MY FAVORITE GOLF CLUB! I'M AFRAID I CAN'T LET YOU HAVE IT!

WE NEED THAT HAT, OR WE'LL BE STUCK DOWN HERE FOREVER!

YOU GOT ANYTHING WE MIGHT BE ABLE TO TRADE HIM FOR IT?

ALL'S I GOT IS MY LUCKY YO-YO.

GREAT! I'LL BUY YOU A NEW ONE WHEN WE GET BACK!

WELL, YOUR HIGHNESS... WHY SETTLE FOR A SIMPLE GOLF-CLUB COVER WHEN YOU COULD TRADE IT FOR THIS SPLENDIFEROUS LUCKY YO-YO?

WHY, WITH THIS YO-YO, YOU CAN DO TRICKS LIKE THIS DOUBLE-INSIDE HOT-DOG FRENCH SWIRL! READY? WATCH!

THUD.

UH, NO THANKS...

...I'LL PASS.

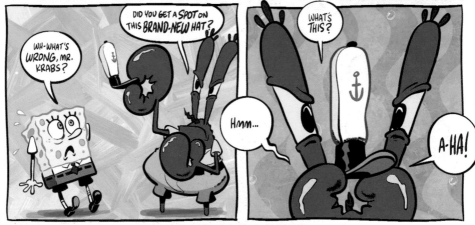

Story, penciling, and lettering: Sherm Cohen. Inks: Vince Deporter. Coloring: Digital Chameleon. *SpongeBob SquarePants* created by Stephen Hillenburg.

BEFORE WE CONFRONT SNORELONN, WE SHOULD SEARCH THE CRIME SCENE FOR INCRIMINATING EVIDENCE.

THIS PIE LOOKS PRETTY INCRIMINATING! CHOMP! CHOMP!

WHAT'S THIS?

OUR ENEMY IS CRAFTIER THAN I THOUGHT! HE'LL PROBABLY TRY TO STICK THIS IN YOUR EAR AND SUCK YOUR BRAINS OUT OF YOUR SKULL!

I DON'T HAVE ANY EARS.

YOU DON'T? HOW CAN YOU HEAR WHAT I'M SAYING?

WHAT? I CAN'T HEAR YOU.

I SAID, "HOW CAN YOU HEAR WHAT I'M SAYING?"

WHAT?

HOW CAN YOU--

OH, FORGET IT.

OKAY.

WE MUST BE CAUTIOUS... RUMOR HAS IT THAT SNORELONN LIKES TO EAT HIS VICTIMS!

WAIT--THIS BOOK! IT--IT'S HORRIBLE! THIS BOOK... ≥GULP!≤ IT'S...IT'S...

IT'S A COOKBOOK! AAAAUGH!

101 Lite RECIPES

RECIPES

THEY AIN'T AFRAID OF NO GHOSTS!

THE REAL GHOSTBUSTERS

A Hard Day's Fright

COMING SOON FROM TITAN BOOKS ·